CELTIC

INSPIRATIONS

CELTIC

INSPIRATIONS

ESSENTIAL MEDITATIONS

AND TEXTS

LYN WEBSTER WILDE

DUNCAN BAIRD PUBLISHERS

LONDON

Celtic Inspirations

For Rebecca and Christian, with love and gratitude

Distributed in the USA and Canada by
Sterling Publishing Co., Inc.
387 Park Avenue South
New York, NY 10016-8810

This edition first published in the UK and USA in 2004 by
Duncan Baird Publishers Ltd
Sixth Floor, Castle House
75–76 Wells Street
London W1T 3QH

Editor: James Hodgson
Managing Designer: Dan Sturges
Designer: Gail Jones
Picture Researcher: Susannah Stone
Commissioned artworks: Peter Visscher

Library of Congress Cataloging-in-Publication Data Available

ISBN-13: 978-1-84483-099-2   ISBN-10: 1-84483-099-3
10 9 8 7 6 5 4 3

Typeset in Perpetua and Caslon Open Face
Color reproduction by Scanhouse, Malaysia
Printed in China by Imago

CONTENTS

INTRODUCTION

A cauldron adorned with a horned god, riddling tales of shapeshifters and magical animals, knotwork with no beginning or end, golden torcs glinting on the necks of fierce warriors, noble knights on a Grail quest – these are images of the Celts which haunt us today. Their great myths and stories – of King Arthur, St Brigit, Cuchulainn, Boudicca – still enchant. The bard Taliesin took his inspiration from the cauldron of the goddess Cerridwen: this book is a kind of cauldron too – stir it, taste its magical liquor, and you will find inspiration to illuminate your day and tackle the riddles of your own life.

The Celtic imagination

In the modern world it is easy to lose the connection with the source of creativity in ourselves. The need to earn a living, the temptations of materialism, anxiety about the future, can all conspire to make us contract and become fearful. The Celts invite us to flow, to circle, to expand, to explore. They knew that alongside the ordinary world there was a magical realm full of

possibilities which could be entered by anyone who knew the right way. They called it the Otherworld (see box below). This book offers you the keys to this special place.

The treasures of the Celtic imagination can be found scattered throughout the art, literature and folklore. Many of the spirals, triskeles (three-legged motifs) and fantastic beasts which we see so often in Celtic decoration originated in the illuminated gospels made by monks in the seventh and eighth centuries AD. The *Mabinogion* – a collection of Welsh tales written down in the Middle Ages – belongs to a much older oral tradition. It contains much fascinating material about the pre-Christian gods, and

The Otherworld

The Celtic Otherworld is the world of the imagination, of dream and trance, where usual rules do not apply. Sometimes it is portrayed as a blessed and bliss-ful place, where there is no time and no suffering, only beauty, fine music and delight. Sometimes it appears as a darker, more ambiguous realm, but never as a grisly hell or a place of eternal retribution. You may stumble into it by chance, or be lured, often by an Otherworld woman. And remember: never make love with an Otherworld being or eat their food – or you may find yourself trapped there.

it has intriguing early versions of the Arthurian legends.

From Ireland there is a rich vein of poetry and tales, such as *The Voyage of Bran*, which takes us to an Otherworld of enchanted islands where "the sea horses glisten", and the comical *Cattle Raid of Cooley*, which tells of an epic battle between two bulls.

Oral traditions have been kept alive by folklorists like Alexander Carmichael who, in his anthology the *Carmina Gadelica*, collected ancient Scottish songs and tales before they were lost for ever.

Who were the Celts?

The Celts emerged into history in the millennium before the birth of Christ when they began to spread from their homelands in central Europe east toward Turkey and Greece, west toward Germany, France, Britain and Ireland, and south into Italy and Spain. They were a vigorous, warlike people, skilled in metalworking and horsemanship, and keen to trade. They had a distinctive curvilinear artistic style which they used on both weapons and items of personal adornment. Rich graves found in their homelands in Austria and Switzerland show that this was a sophisticated society with strong links to the classical world.

By the fourth century BC the Celts dominated northern Europe. The

Romans challenged their expansion and invaded both Gaul (France) and Britain to plant their own colonies. According to Julius Caesar the Celts were a vital, child-like people who liked colourful clothes and plenty to drink, and were brave and reckless in battle. He admired them in certain ways, but still considered them to be barbarians whose civilization was much inferior to his own. The Celts fought bitterly

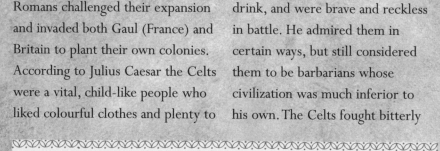

The Celtic journey

There is a tradition in Celtic literature of immrama — *stories of sea voyages in which the hero visits various enchanted islands, each with its own supernatural inhabitants or qualities, usually including one ruled by seductive women. These tales often have a spiritual significance as well as being exciting and entertaining. They are an example of how the Celtic imagination entwines two or more threads of meaning into one story, in order to disguise and yet adorn the truth.*

Do not fall on a bed of sloth,
Let not intoxication overcome you;
Begin a voyage over the clear sea,
And perchance you may reach the land of women.

(FROM *The Voyage of Bran*)

against the Romans, including several battles in which they were led by the warrior queen, Boudicca. There was a heroic last stand at Anglesey, but the Celts eventually lost and had to accept the Roman colonization of their lands.

However, the Romans were gracious in victory, respecting Celtic cultural traditions. Many of these survived in various forms until waves of new invaders – Angles, Saxons, Jutes, Vikings – arrived and suppressed them more brutally. Some Celtic peoples were absorbed into the culture of the invaders, some fled west to Wales and Cornwall. The Romans never conquered Ireland, so the Celtic culture remained pure there until the coming of the Vikings toward the end of the eighth century. As a result, early Irish literature is one of the richest sources of information about the Celts.

Nowadays, people of Celtic origin have spread all over the world, particularly to North America, Australia and New Zealand. Sometimes their culture survives in a remarkably pure form: there are Gaelic-speaking communities in Nova Scotia in Canada and Welsh speakers in Argentina. Celtic art and music are enjoying a spectacular renaissance as people begin to recognize that they represent a vital part of Europe's ancient native tradition – as rich as that of the Native Americans in America or the aboriginal peoples in Australia.

Celtic spirituality

Long before the Celts swept westward, the native peoples of Europe embodied their knowledge of the sun, moon and stars in monuments such as Stonehenge in England, Newgrange in Ireland and the Ring of Brodgar in Orkney (Scotland). When the Celts came, there was a reservoir of native wisdom for them to tap into and make their own. The bards and druids carried on the wisdom tradition, and the stone circles were incorporated into Celtic tales and ceremonies.

Early writings show that, on the western seaboard at least, the Celtic gods and goddesses were grouped into various families, such as the "Children of Don", known in Ireland as the "Tuatha Dé Danaan", and the "Children of Llyr". Many Celtic tales tell of these gods: Don, or in Ireland Danu, the great mother goddess who gives her name to many of the rivers of Europe, such as the Dnieper and the Don; the magical child Lleu, or Lugh, who grows up to become a solar hero; Manannan mac Llyr, the sea god, equivalent of the Greek deity Poseidon (the Isle of Man is named after him); Arianrhod, the shining virgin goddess whose castle – Corona Borealis – can be seen among the stars; Bran the Blessed, the great king who sacrifices his head in order to save his land; and Morgan, or the Morrigan, the dark goddess who haunts the battlefields in the

shape of a black crow to collect the souls of the dead. These deities are found all over the Celtic world with slight variations and under different names. When the Romans came it often happened that their gods merged with the Celtic ones, and names were changed again.

With the coming of Christianity many of the Druidic wizards converted to the new faith. As a part of the same process, some of the old gods were transformed into saints: for example, the triple goddess Brigid became St Brigit. This religion, with its emphasis on love and individual salvation, appealed to the Celtic spirit, and a golden age of Celtic Christianity arose: great men like Columba founded

monasteries, most notably Iona, and the exquisite illuminated gospels, such as those from Lindisfarne and Kells, were created.

True Celtic spirituality is neither pagan nor Christian but something that transcends these categories. It is based on a deep connection with the natural world, a relentless intellectual curiosity and a sense of comradeship with all creatures. The Arthurian legends, which are of Celtic origin, weave these strands into the world-famous story of Arthur and Guinevere, and their court at Camelot. Their doomed love, the coming of the wasteland and the quest for the Grail, which brings regeneration and hope, are all quintessentially Celtic themes.

THE CELTIC
TREASURE CHEST

Hidden within the Celtic heritage is a treasure chest of mystical techniques and traditions which can still be explored today. It was – and is – a deeply magical culture, which sees men and women as creative beings who work with the divine forces, not as passive subjects who simply do what they are told. The ability to see into the future, to use augury to find what is lost, to cast benevolent spells, to interpret dreams, were all part of daily life. Sometimes the native druidical magic clashed with Christian beliefs, but there are also instances where the Christians borrowed from the old magic and used it to enhance their own vision.

BEYOND THE VISIBLE

For the Celts the visible world was interpenetrated by an invisible "otherworld" of elemental beings and gods. Mountains or hills were the abode of the sky god, and sacred to him under his various names – Lleu, Bel and, later, St Michael. Trees connected the upper and lower worlds, and rivers were often named after the goddesses, such as Don and Verbeia, who brought the waters of life to mankind.

Sensing the landscape

The Celts sensed the presence of their gods everywhere – in mist hanging over a valley, trees sighing in a gale, or rain turning meadow to lake overnight.

Landscape and weather were the fabric of their lives, and to be weather-wise was crucial for survival. This may be why the Celts had such a keen awareness of the supernatural: enlivening the physical senses also awakens the subtle antennae of the spirit.

If you are curious about what lies beyond the visible, first tune in to the physical world. Get out more, even in the cold or wet. Walk. Watch. Stop and listen. Notice how you feel. The Otherworld may have opened its gates.

SPELLS AND INCANTATIONS

In the hard, often dangerous world of the Celts, a fearless and hopeful outlook was essential. Working in a similar way to modern affirmations, spells and incantations were a means of instilling a positive attitude. The incantation below is from the *Carmina Gadelica* – a collection of Scottish songs, prayers and verses in which Christian and Pagan elements mingle gracefully.

I shall not be killed,
I shall not be harried,
I shall not be put in cell,
I shall not be wounded,
Neither shall Christ leave me
* in forgetfulness,*
No fire, no sun, no moon shall burn me,

No water, no loch, no sea shall drown me,
No arrow of fairy or dart of fay shall
* wound me,*
And I under the protection of
* Holy Mary,*
And my gentle foster mother,
* my beloved Bride.*

In this beautiful incantation of protection you can hear a typically Celtic note: there is no entreaty or prayer, only a serene confidence in the power of the Virgin Mary and Bride, the Scottish name for St Brigit, who was called the "foster-mother of Christ" by the Gaels.

A spell of protection

Before entering a challenging or threatening situation, make up a short incantation, using your own words and tailoring them to your circumstances. Make sure the words are affirmative, not negative, and repeat them as often as you can, under your breath if necessary, because spells gain power from repetition. Your mood will lighten and even the most difficult situation will become more bearable. Below is an example.

As I enter this place of healing to visit
*   my mother*
I know that both she and I are protected
By angels and, no matter what,
All will be well and they will be there
To hold us and connect us
With the powers of healing and peace.

Divinatory spells

The child's rhyme about magpies "One for sorrow, two for joy" is a remnant of the old Celtic tradition of augury, known in Scotland as the *frith*. Many techniques depended on observing the pattern of flight of birds, often by making fists, holding them to your eyes and looking up through the gap between them.

There is a Gaelic tale of Mary using augury to find the boy Christ when she lost him in the Temple. This helped the Celts reconcile the Pagan origins of divination with their Christian beliefs.

An augury to find what is lost
You will need a small collection of different feathers, which you have found yourself while out walking. Sit at a table, clear a space in front of you and hold the feathers. For a moment bring to your mind a vivid picture of the thing that you have lost. Then shut your eyes and allow your mind to soar with the birds whose feathers you hold, up into the empty sky. Keeping your eyes shut, stroke the feathers and lay them out in a pattern that feels right. When you open your eyes the pattern before you will show you where to look for what you have lost. Good luck!

THE WISDOM OF THE SWORD

Swords were not just weapons of war for the Celts but had profound symbolic and magical significance. The bard Amergin said, "I am the point of a weapon", meaning that the piercing power of truth was in his words. The Sword of Nuadu, one of the four "hallows", or treasures, brought to Ireland by the Tuatha Dé Danaan, "the children of the Goddess Danu", inflicted wounds that could never be healed. Paradoxically, a sword was able to heal the land when wielded by a noble warrior or wise king. Arthur used his sword Excalibur to protect his realm from the evil forces that wished to destroy it. The sword can be seen as the symbol of the necessary action that saves the day.

The sword of decision

The two sides of a sword can be seen as the two sides of a dispute or argument and the point as the clear decision which resolves the tension and reawakens your energy. The edge of a sword can also be used to cut connections that are binding you or draining your energy.

1 If you need to sever your links with someone, or break old, outmoded habits so that new ones may arise, take a long knife (or sword if you have one) and clean it.

2 Stand in a clear space with the knife or sword ready. Bring to mind what links you with the other person or what attracts you to the old habit. Try to sense the link in your body as well as your mind. If you are breaking away from a person, thank them for all that they have given and taught you.

3 Make a clean downward sweep with the knife or sword to cut the link. You may need to perform this exercise on up to three occasions to make a complete break.

RIDDLES

The bard Taliesin framed his mystical insights in riddling verse that hinted at a reality too big and too slippery for the normal mind to grasp. He could not say directly what he meant — he needed to stretch the imagination of his listeners to lead them to the truth. Indeed, this was one of the roles of the bard: to convey secret or sacred knowledge in verse.

An elementary riddle

Can you identify the "strong creature" in this riddle by Taliesin?

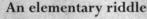

Discover thou what is
The strong creature from before
* the flood,*
Without flesh, without bone,
Without vein, without blood,
Without head, without feet,
It will neither be older nor younger
Than at the beginning.

The riddle of the cauldron

Now try to answer this question, often asked of apprentice druids: "What two words are never spoken from the cauldron?" (A clue: the cauldron contains the waters of life, which never stop moving …)

Such riddles are like Zen koans (paradoxes) — the key is to think about them, even if you don't get the "right" answer.

(Taliesin's "strong creature" is the wind, and the two words are "be still!")

CLAIRVOYANCE

Among the Celts there have always been "fey" people, who are said to have "the sight". In the old days it was thought that they consorted with fairies who gave them their gift. Clairvoyance stemmed from a world-view in which everything is connected, in which the boundaries between one person and another, between past and future, seem to melt. When this gift was misused, it was called witchcraft, but when used wisely it was much valued.

St Columba of Iona was among those who had been granted the sight. On one occasion he sent an angel to catch a monk whom he could see, in his mind's eye, falling from a tower.

From the *Life of St Columba* by Adamnan

*"There are some, though very few, who are enabled by divine grace to see most clearly
and distinctly the whole compass of the world, and to embrace within their own
wondrously enlarged mental capacity the utmost limits of the heavens and the earth
at the same moment, as if all were illuminated by a single ray of the sun."*

The journey to the centre

To clarify your mind and develop
your clairvoyant skills, contemplate
the classic Celtic spirals below,
which are to be found on the
Aberlemno stone in Scotland.

See how, from the zero point in
the centre, in one case three, and in
the other four, spiralling black
threads weave the whole pattern.

Consider the spirals as Celtic
meditation mandalas. Their
marvellous, flowing symmetry
calms the mind and takes it to
the simple, quiet space where
clear-seeing can occur.

INTUITION

S t Brigit had great powers of intuition: a woman brought her mute daughter to the saint for healing, and Brigit asked the girl if she wanted to marry or to be a nun. "She won't answer, you know," interrupted the mother, but Brigit took the girl's hand and said she wouldn't let go until she got a reply. "I don't want anything except what you want," blurted the girl, who had never spoken a word before. Brigit sensed that she had to break the mother's control over the child and connect with her directly. Intuition works at a deeper level than words.

Tuning into other people

We are all capable of empathy. Use this simple exercise to help you sense how someone else is feeling.

1 Ask the person to stop talking and, sitting opposite them, bring your breathing into rhythm with theirs. Observe their posture and mirror it with your own. Notice how you feel, sitting and breathing in this way.

2 You may then be able to ask the person a question which will allow their true feelings to emerge. Make sure you are looking into their eyes when they give their answer.

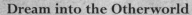

DREAM AND REALITY

To the Celts, dreams were a magical reflection of reality, a natural path into the Otherworld. In the Irish tale *The Dream of Angus*, Angus dreams of a girl who comes to the end of his bed and plays music. He falls in love and after a long, magical journey he finds her, wins her and the dream becomes real.

Dream into the Otherworld

Like Angus, we can use our dreams as bridges to the Otherworld.

If you experience a vivid dream, try recreating it in a drawing or painting. This may open up a channel to your unconscious.

If a dream ends badly, stay in bed in a drowsy but alert state and re-run the dream, this time allowing a positive outcome to occur. Don't force the result: you can't ram your way into the Otherworld.

If you experience a strong feeling in a dream – exhilaration, freedom, erotic pleasure – then look for ways to recreate it in waking life. Dreams often give glimpses of hidden possibilities, which need to be nurtured if they are to become real.

The welcome intruder

At night we drop
Our shields and veils.
Manannan, god of sea and dreams,
Speaks in his secret voice.

DREAM INCUBATION

The old tales contain traces of a tradition of dream incubation among the Celts which is now lost. In an Irish tale, a man wants to dream who will become the next king, so he prepares by eating the flesh of a sacrificed bull, drinking its broth and having a special incantation of truth sung over him while he sleeps.

A Scottish version of this custom, which endured until the seventeenth century, has the dreamer wrap himself in the hide of a newly slain deer and lie out in the open, fasting, for two or three nights, until the special dream comes.

Such bloody customs are no longer appealing, but the principle of inducing a certain type of dream can still be applied in modern times.

Ask for a special dream

To seek inspiration from your unconscious, try following these steps every night until the special dream arrives.

1 Avoid alcohol and heavy food during the evening. Make sure that your bedroom is quiet, clean and uncluttered and place a pen and some paper next to your bed.

2 When you lie down to sleep, repeat several times "Tonight I intend to dream about …".

3 As soon as you wake, write down any images or thoughts that are in your mind, even if you're unsure whether you dreamed them.

INNER JOURNEYS

In Scottish fishing communities, if a boat was lost and fishermen drowned it was important for their families to discover the resting place of their loved ones. There was one way to find out. The families would seek a virgin woman of sound mind and body. She would lie down and go to sleep. Her spirit would leave her body and search for the ship. When the spirit returned and the woman woke up, she would give a report of what had happened to the ship and the men on it. This inner journey was as dangerous as a voyage at sea: if the wind changed while the woman was out of her body, she risked losing her wits.

Tuning into the web

If you are worried about a friend or a member of your family who is far away from you and facing illness, danger or any other form of adversity, you can make a storm-proof inner journey to support and encourage them.

1 Imagine that you are sitting face to face with the person you want to help.

2 Look into their eyes and say some words of protection. Use your own words or recite one of the Celtic blessings shown opposite.

The Three be about thy head
The Three be about thy breast,
The Three be about thy body
Each night and each day,
In the encompassment of the Three
Throughout thy life long.

    (FROM THE *Carmina Gadelica*)

The shield of Michael be over thee
King of the bright angels
To shield thee and to guard thee
From thy summit to thy sole.

    (FROM THE *Carmina Gadelica*)

May the Lord bless you
May the Lady hold you
May the Angels
protect you.

    (MODERN CELTIC BLESSING)

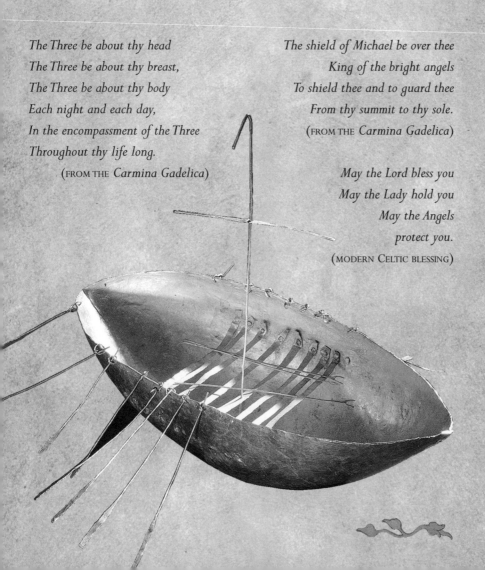

WANDERINGS

I n the forest we wander, lost and confused, trying to find our path or at least a clue to it. In the *Quest of the San Graal*, Arthur's knights pursue their search in the dense forest of Broceliande, meeting dark and deadly antagonists, seductive, treacherous maidens, monstrous dragons – all the hidden powers of the unconscious. In the forest they will eventually find what they seek, but only after they have been purified by pain and suffering. It seems we must lose ourselves to find ourselves, but we are frightened to let go. Once we are humbled, exhausted – maybe even once we have given up – we may be ready to stumble into the Grail Chapel.

DARKNESS AND LIGHT

I n the mysterious eighth-century saga *The Voyage of Maelduin*, a group of sailors come upon an extraordinary island. It is divided in two by a fence: on one side there are white sheep and on the other black. If the island's shepherd throws a black sheep into the white half, it turns white and a white sheep turns black in the black half. The Celts understood that "black-and-white thinking" is unhelpful, and that many apparently negative situations can be perceived in a positive way. The key is to avoid becoming entrenched in extreme points of view.

A break in the clouds

When confronted by a testing problem, we tend to think in extremes – we imagine we must do something drastic or difficult to break the deadlock. But the truly skilful action often lies in finding a middle way – which is not the same thing as a compromise.

Therefore, when considering a course of action, look for the small, seemingly insignificant shift of attitude or thinking that has the power to tip the balance. You'll know when you've hit upon the right idea because it will come accompanied by a sigh of relief and recognition.

BARDS, DRUIDS AND SEERS

Celtic society had great respect for those who could see beyond the visible and use their special powers for the benefit of others. These wise and gifted people might have had a public role as druid priests and lawgivers or as bards who held in their memory the history of their clan – or they might have been humbler "cunning" men or women who practised natural lore relating to health, childbirth or agriculture. Many of these skills hark back to the mysterious practices of even earlier times, when shamans would travel to the Otherworld to bring healing to the people and the land.

SPECIAL POWERS

O ruids were not just priests, but highly trained philosophers, magicians, lawmakers, astrologers and astronomers. Bards and poet-seers were also trained intensively. Bards had to be able to recite the past deeds of their clan, enchant their public with the old tales and invent verses full of riddling meanings and occult lore. Seers had an uncanny gift: they would see the doubles or "fetches" of living people, which was a sign that they would soon die.

Druids and trees

*The word "druid" may be derived from the old Celtic words for oak tree ("duir")
and knowledge ("wid"). The oak was considered to be the prime gateway or "door"
to sacred knowledge. In another association with trees, Caesar noted that the
druids usually met in woodland groves. To induce prophetic visions they would
sleep on "wattles of knowledge", platforms or cages made of woods such as rowan
(sacred to the triple-goddess Brigid, and used as a protection against enchant-
ment) or hazel, the tree whose nuts fed the salmon of knowledge (see p.44).*

Julius Caesar on the druids

We owe much of what we know today about the early Celts to the legacy of classical Greek and Roman writers, including the historians Pliny and Strabo and, above all, the great military leader Julius Caesar. Caesar kept a detailed account of the Roman conquest of Gaul (modern-day France). During the campaign he observed the druids at first hand:

"They are concerned with religious matters, perform sacrifices … and interpret omens. Young people go to them to be educated and they are held in high honour … . They debate concerning the heavens, the movement of the stars, the size of the universe and the earth, the workings of nature and of the immortal gods … ."

BECOMING A SEER

The gift of the "sight" was highly valued by the Celts. But this gift could cause the possessor great sorrow — especially if he or she foresaw the death of someone close to them. On the other hand, the seer might be able to avert catastrophe after receiving a premonition of danger.

The most famous seer in Irish mythology was Finn, whose name means "wise or knowing one". It was said that he gained his special ability while cooking a salmon: he accidentally burned his finger and stuck it in his mouth. Instantly he knew everything in the world, because the salmon was the salmon of knowledge, which had eaten nine hazelnuts from the tree of wisdom hanging over a magic pool in the Otherworld.

A different point of view

When you turn around
It is always behind you.
But with the back of your head
You can see it clearly.

Find your hidden knowledge

If you are grappling with a problem, you may benefit from a completely fresh approach. Try this ancient Celtic seer's technique.

1 Collect some natural objects that appeal to you, such as stones, twigs, leaves, feathers or crystals. Put them into a bag and, holding the question you want answered in your mind, draw out one object. This represents your answer.

2 The meaning will not be clear immediately, but don't look for a rational analysis. Instead carry the object with you and contemplate it whenever you can. When you least expect it, the answer may emerge.

BECOMING A BARD

The training to become a bard or *file* (an Irish poet-seer) was long and arduous: it could involve lying in a dark hut for hours, or sitting in cold water to force inspiration to come. But a poet had to have natural talent before he could be trained. There are many tales of the favoured one receiving his gift from a woman of the Otherworld, as in the Scottish border ballad of Thomas the Rhymer:

> *Then they came to a garden green,*
> *And she pulled an apple from a tree:*
> *"Take this for your wages, true Thomas;*
> *It will give you the tongue that can never lie"*

It is the queen of Elfland who initiates Thomas and gives him the gift of unfailing truthfulness. He is not sure he wants this, because he realizes how awkward it could be when flirting with women or haggling at the market, but she insists. Every great gift must have its price.

Kindle your creative spark

We all have great potential for creativity. This bardic exercise will help you to kindle your spark.

1 Find a room that can be made completely dark and quiet. Sit or lie comfortably wrapped in a blanket and wait until midnight.

2 Keep your eyes open and stay there until you are teetering right on the edge of sleep. In this trance-like state, which is neither sleeping nor waking, new ideas will bubble into your mind.

3 Get up and write your thoughts down straightaway (however odd they may seem) – otherwise you'll forget them. They may be the seeds of something wonderful.

GLIMPSING THE OTHERWORLD

In an old Welsh tale, Pwyll, the Prince of Dyfed, is out hunting with his hounds when he encounters another pack of hounds, of weird appearance, bringing down a stag: "… their hair was of a brilliant shining white, and their ears were red: and as the whiteness of their bodies shone, so did the redness of their ears glisten." Then the owner of these hounds appears and it is none other than Arawn, king of the Otherworld, who persuades Pwyll to swap places with him for a year. While in the Otherworld, Pwyll wins the beautiful Rhiannon as his wife.

A brush with the Otherworld

There are many signs that an entrance to the Otherworld is near — time may distort, and often an animal with bright eyes will look at you or invite you to follow it.

Go out either at dawn or at dusk. Walk slowly, in silence; stop, look and listen. You are searching for a creature — a bird, mouse, squirrel, badger or even a fellow human — who will guide you to the Otherworld. You'll know when you've arrived: there'll be a deep silence and colours will become more vivid. Remember, it is a subtle, evanescent place. You cannot stay there for long.

PERILS OF THE OTHERWORLD

The magical Otherworld holds great treasures, and brings inspiration to those who visit it, but it can be dangerous to linger there too long. In the *Mabinogion*, Rhiannon and her son Pryderi are trapped there when their hands become frozen to a golden bowl suspended from the sky by chains. They suffer like beasts of burden until they are saved by their friends. In the Scottish ballad of Tam Lin, the eponymous hero is rescued from "elfland" by his true love, Janet, who has to hold onto him while he mutates into various fierce creatures and perilous objects, such as a lion, a bear and a red-hot rod of iron. It takes patience and practice to travel safely in the Otherworld.

Keep an Otherworld journal

We cannot stay in otherworldly creative states of consciousness for long, and we tend to forget them once they have passed. So it is a good idea to keep a journal in which to record the ideas, objects and experiences you encounter on your visits to the Otherworld.

1 Record vivid perceptions, mystical experiences, wise insights, flashes of inspiration and startling images in your Otherworld journal in words or pictures. Don't worry about your draughtsmanship or how elegantly you express yourself.

2 Include anything else that inspires you. It might be a poem, quotation, newspaper cutting or photograph, or something from the natural world.

3 Review and update your journal regularly. Its contents will percolate into your psyche and breathe life into your creative projects.

SHAPESHIFTING

The idea of shapeshifting is deeply embedded in Celtic culture. In a famous poem, the *Song of Amergin*, Amergin lists his numerous mystical incarnations, including the following:

> *I am the roar of the ocean*
> *I am a powerful ox*
> *I am a hawk on a cliff*
> *I am a salmon in pools*
> *I am a lake in a plain*

In many stories we read of people being transformed into birds or animals, which may be a memory of shamanic rites from pre-Christian times. In the tale *Math, Son of Mathonwy*, two brothers, Gwydion and Gilfaethwy, rape a maiden from their uncle's court. As a punishment their uncle, who is a magician, changes them in turn into wolves, pigs and deer and tells them that they must mate with each other and produce offspring before they can be restored to human form and forgiven.

Find the animal within you
When you are in a relaxed and
playful mood, try a simple form
of shapeshifting that will give you
a new perspective on a different
species of animal – or perhaps an
individual animal, such as your
pet cat or dog – and enliven your
relationship with that creature.

1 Study your chosen animal
closely. Walk or sit like it; mirror
its actions, sounds and expressions;
move at its pace, not your own.

2 Imagine looking at the world
through the animal's eyes.
Where do its hazards lie?
What would it most like
to do at this moment.
Use all your senses
to explore your
surroundings.

3 If you have
adopted the shape of
a tame animal, finish by
playing with it as if you
were both of the same species.

TIME TRAVEL

The Celts took over Neolithic grave mounds (such as Gavrinis in Brittany or Newgrange in Ireland) and used them for their own rites and ceremonies. Called "the hollow hills", they were believed to be gateways to the Otherworld. Anyone spending the night alone on one of these mounds could spiral to the place beyond time where their ancestors lived – or even, perhaps, to the land of their future descendants.

The spiral way

The spiral shell of the snail is an emblem of extraordinary slowness – time moving imperceptibly, like the shaping of the landscape. Yet the spiral (as seen at the great burial mound of Newgrange, illustrated opposite) also suggests the miraculous passage to the Otherworld, a journey that can be made in the twinkling of an eye.

Meditate on the spiral in both these opposing meanings. To fuse these extremes, in an inspired meditation, is to come one step closer to wisdom

Beyond the veil

Only a thin veil separates the living
  from the dead.
In the parallel land of darkness,
  spirits share eternity.

THE POWER OF THREE

The Celts thought, spoke and wrote in threes. Three-pronged statements called triads, such as the one below, encapsulated Celtic wisdom and history in a form that the bards could remember, recite and pass on to their successors. In folk tales the hero or heroine is often granted three wishes; the triple goddess and god arise in many forms; and, underlying all this, is the magical secret about three — it is the first number after one! Because the moment you see one and two you have three, which is the relationship between them. This is the mysterious "third force", which seems invisible but makes all the difference.

The three fortunate concealments of Britain

"The first fortunate concealment: the head of Bran the Blessed, son of Llyr, which was buried in the White Hill in London, with its face toward France ... . Second, the dragons in Dinas Emrys, which Lludd son of Beli concealed; and the third: the bones of Gwerthefyr the Blessed, in the chief ports of this island. And as long as they remained in that concealment, no Saxon oppression would ever come to this island."

Affirming threeness

You can harness the power of three
by making three affirmations at the
beginning of each day. These may
be specific statements of intent
for the day or more general aims
or observations. Express your
affirmations in the positive rather
than the negative. For example:

1 I will get up right now and take
a long walk in the woods before
going to work.

2 I am enjoying my job, especially
the long meetings, which give me a
chance to observe how people are
interacting with each other.

3 My relationship is deepening
gradually and bringing me a great
sense of fulfilment.

THE WISE CHILD

According to the Celts, when a child is born it knows everything and spends the rest of its life forgetting. They embodied this notion in various divine or magical children such as Dylan, Lleu and Finn. The concept of the "wise child" may have stemmed from a belief in reincarnation: children are wise because they hold the distilled experience of their previous lives.

"Old is man when he is born and young, young ever after."

(TALIESIN)

Learn from the young

We often see it as our role to pass on knowledge to children, but there is much that they can teach us.

1 The next time you speak with a small child, listen to what they have to say. Instead of dismissing their view of the world and correcting what you perceive to be their misconceptions, surrender yourself to their curiosity and playfulness.

2 Use a child's way of thinking to tackle problems. Don't edit out any possible solutions, however naïve or far-fetched they may seem, before giving them proper consideration.

DEATH AND REBIRTH

The chambered tomb of Gavrinis (opposite) stands on a lonely "isle of the dead" off the coast of Brittany. Its walls are engraved with patterns that have puzzled archeologists for centuries. One theory is that, as part of an initiation ceremony, candidates were shut in the tomb. In their terror, they would have traced the spirals on the walls with their fingers, and would eventually have been "reborn" with a new understanding of reality, having lost their fear of death. Often we have to stop clinging onto our old ways before we can reach out for the new.

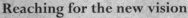

Reaching for the new vision

You probably don't want to be shut in a tomb for days, but a "retreat" from your everyday routine is essential if you need to make changes in your life.

Go somewhere new for at least 24 hours – ideally longer. Leave behind your mobile phone (cellphone) and stay away from radio and TV. Seek silence. Consider what you need to let go of and visualize the future you desire. Draw pictures and write poems based on this vision.

When you go home the world will seem different and you will feel inspired and energized to make the necessary changes.

BODY, SKY
AND LANDSCAPE

The Celts had an intimate relationship with the land: their landscape was a living being. The hills and fertile valleys were the body of the goddess, great ripples of rock under grass were the muscles of the dragon, rushing rivers were the arteries of the earth-giant. In the night sky the moon, whose phases dictated when crops should be planted, sailed through shifting constellations of stars which were the homes of gods and goddesses, such as Gwydion, Arianrhod and their mother Don. All the natural cosmos, both earthly and celestial, spoke the profound language of myth.

THE LANDSCAPE OF MYTH

For the Celts the outer reflected the inner, and certain places held a strong emotional charge. The sea was the cauldron which gave and took life; beaches were the border between this world and the Otherworld (or the conscious and the unconscious); the mythical islands visited in the voyage poems each embodied a particular state of consciousness. Hills or mountains gave closer access to the world of the sky gods. And under the earth was the world where the fairies and gnomes ruled.

The elemental world of the fairies

The Celtic fairy could be a dangerous creature who would steal your baby and replace it with a sickly changeling, or put a hex on your cattle. On the other hand, in Ireland, the Tuatha Dé Danaan (Children of the Goddess Danu) were tall shining beings with magical skills who lived in another dimension inside the "hollow hills". It is the fairies who create the natural world. And any enchanted place will be the haunt of elemental spirits, if only you have eyes to see them.

EARTH ENERGY

The Celts sited their temples carefully to exploit the energies of the earth. For example, a shrine to Manannan, the Lord of the Waters, might be built near a river. Certain places held certain kinds of power, depending on factors such as the stone underlying them, the kinds of vegetation growing, and the positioning of nearby hills or waterways. Some places are healing, some energizing, some conducive to contemplation; while some have an uncomfortable or uncanny atmosphere.

The art of dowsing

Dowsing is an ancient method of detecting subtle currents of earth energy, such as underground water. A common technique involves holding a forked rod, usually made of hazel, in both hands with the single end pointing toward the ground. You should feel a reaction when you walk across a channel of energy – it might be a tingle in your hands, a twitching of the rod or a light vibration.

It's important to feel relaxed, so prepare by stretching your muscles and breathing deeply. For practice, find a bridge over a river and familiarize yourself with the change in sensation when you move from the bank to the bridge.

THE DRAGON OF THE LAND

The "dragon of the land" arises where natural contours create an aura of coiled power and majesty — where the landscape heaves and swirls like a creature rising from the crust of the earth. Ancient tribes sometimes celebrated this power by cutting out figures in the ground or by building spiral terracing or ramparts. At the White Horse of Uffington in Oxfordshire there used to be a yearly "scouring" of the outline of the horse, as well as a downhill cheese-rolling competition — both ways of marking the special impact of this dragon place.

Harness the dragon power

Wherever the shape of the land makes you think of a mighty beast, use this method to absorb its power.

1 Walk over the ground. Notice how the energy travels up your body, to your pelvis, stomach, heart and head. Then be aware of your whole body as an organ for perceiving the dragon power.

2 Do a dragon-dance by stamping clockwise around the most powerful spot. When you have finished you will feel energized, having made a strong connection with the dragon of the land.

TREE WISDOM

The Celtic landscape was far more heavily forested than most parts of our own, and so it's not surprising that Celtic culture was saturated with tree lore. The first Celtic alphabet was Ogham, a system of strokes across a horizontal line in which each letter was associated with a tree. The first three letters were Beith (birch), Luis (rowan) and Nuin (ash).

The wood from each tree was accorded a practical, medicinal and symbolic value. The slim and elegant birch, whose silvery bark could be made into shoes, baskets and boats, was seen as a female tree, associated with the "Lady of the Woods". It was used to treat rheumatism and, in magic spells, to promote fertility. The yew, often found in churchyards, was linked with death and rebirth, and was used to make longbows. However, because it was poisonous, it was not used medicinally.

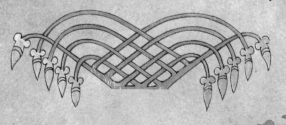

Choose the willow of the streams,
Choose the hazel of the rocks,
Choose the alder of the marshes,
Choose the birch of the waterfalls.

Choose the ash of the shade,
Choose the yew of resilience,
Choose the elm of the brae,
Choose the oak of the sun.

(FROM THE *Carmina Gadelica*)

Make a wand

Wands serve as a tangible symbol of your connection with the natural world. Here's how to make one.

1 Take a walk in the woods to look for a tree with which you feel an affinity. Locate a slender branch suitable for making a rod or staff.

2 Ask the tree whether you may take the branch. If the answer is "yes", then saw or break it, cut it to size, and strip the bark. If you like you can also carve your wand.

3 Carry your wand when you go out walking – over time it may start to feel like a part of your body.

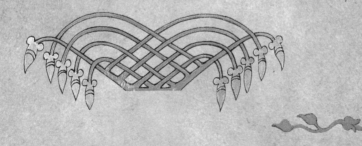

WATER'S HEALING POWERS

ater had a special magic for the Celts as a symbol of vitality and inspiration. The fact that it could capture light (for example, a reflection of the setting sun) could not be rationally explained and was taken as proof of supernatural properties. Wells and springs were charged with magic powers. Lakes and rivers were the dwelling-places of otherworldly beings, like the Lady of the Lake in Arthurian legend.

Walking by a river or stream, let the power of water, seen and heard, energize your spirit. Let every ripple add its soothing blessing to your deepening inner calm.

The watery cage of the moon
Do not fear the Druid's magic.
You too are a skilled magician.
You can summon the spirits of the night.
You can ensnare the moon in a puddle.

If you gaze into a puddle and see the full moon's reflection there, the time is auspicious for you to make a wish — as long as your wish is sincere and virtuous, there is a good chance that it will be realized soon. But best of all is to try to catch the moon's reflection in a well: this simple spell may bring you closer to achieving your heart's desire.

HEALING HERBS

Plants had a vital medicinal role in Celtic life and myth. In Irish mythology, the great physician Dian Cecht killed his son Miach out of jealousy at his son's superior medical skills. Magically, 365 healing herbs grew out of Miach's grave.

Some of the herbs that feature in the old tales can still work their spell today. Meadowsweet was used to calm the hero Cuchulainn when he went mad, and it was one of the plants that the magicians Math and Gwydion used to make the Woman of Flowers, Blodeuedd. It served as an air freshener, and was used to flavour mead (hence the name). Like aspirin, meadowsweet contains salicylic acid, so it also helps to alleviate headaches.

A meadowsweet infusion

You can make a pleasant tea from the dried flowers and stalks of meadowsweet, which in Europe flowers in July and August. Put a teaspoonful per person into a pot, add boiling water and let it steep for five minutes. You can sweeten it with a little lime-flower honey if you like. This ancient drink (traces have been found in a Bronze Age beaker) is mildly sedative and will ease aches and pains. Drink it as a preparation for sleep.

St John's wort

We now use St John's wort to treat mild depression. For the Celts it was kindling for the sacred Beltane fires, a protection against witchcraft, and excellent cattle feed.

St John's wort, St John's wort
My envy whosoever has thee
I will pluck thee with my right hand
I will preserve thee with my left hand
Whoso findeth thee in the cattle field
Shall never be without kine [cattle].

(FROM THE *Carmina Gadelica*)

HARVESTING COLOUR

The beautiful tartans and plaids we associate with Scotland were coloured with vegetable dyes. In the Highlands sheep's fleeces were put into a three-legged cauldron in layers with crotal moss from the moors and boiled — the result was a bright red fleece (despite the moss being yellow), which could then be spun and woven. For black, oak bark and acorns could be used; for yellow, crab apple or ash; for green, flag iris root. Outside the crofts stood pots for collecting urine, which was used as a mordant (fixative) to prepare the cloth to hold the dye.

A simple dye

This method will work for most plants. Bruise or crush the plant material and put it in a large stainless steel saucepan. Cover with water, bring to the boil and simmer for an hour. Allow the plant to steep in the water for up to three days, stirring it well each day. Strain the liquid through muslin into a dyebath. Add the damp yarn or fabric to the dye-bath. Bring it to the boil and simmer for one hour.

The strength of the dye will depend on what time of day and in what season you picked the plant. For some plants you may need to prepare the cloth with a mordant.

FERTILITY RITES

The pre-Christian Celts had a robust approach to sexuality. If a woman did not conceive with her partner, she could take another lover at the Beltane festival. Many longed-for children must have come from such once-a-year pairings. There were damp, fecund places, such as wells and river sources, where women could go to stimulate their fertility. Couples could also try making love on special spots like the phallus of the Cerne Abbas Giant in Dorset (and this still happens, in spite of the fences!), or anywhere where the landscape mimics the contours of a woman's body, such as the Paps of Anu in Ireland.

A rite of spring
Whether you want to promote fertility of body or of mind, call on the power of the landscape.

1 Choose a juicy green place with bubbling water, or a lush meadow, preferably in spring.

2 Get in contact with the land: roll down a hill, jump up and down or dance – energize your body.

3 When your cells feel enlivened, lie on the ground, naked if you like, and allow yourself to receive the earth and the sky.

THE MOON AND ITS LIGHT

Our ancestors made stone circles to mark the movements and interaction of the sun and moon. They understood that what happens in the heavens affects us on Earth, and saw the moon as a focus for extraterrestrial energies. The Celts believed that when the moon was high it was a good time to plant seeds, while when it was low it was time to harvest (modern biodynamic farmers still apply this rule). Druids would make lunar calculations to advise people when to make a journey or conceive a child. A bronze-age body was found in a grave in England with a disk on its chest with seven notches on it, which may have been used to make such astrological predictions.

Moonlight and moonshadow
Go out at the time of the full moon and walk. Notice the effect of moonlight, how it transforms the world, how strangely bright it is and how strong the moonshadow.

The more time you spend in the moonlight, the more refined your lunar consciousness will become. This will help you become more aware of the rhythms and cycles in the sky and in your own body.

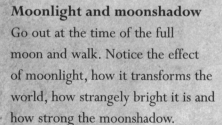

STARLIGHT

When the Welsh Celts looked up at the stars they saw their favourite myths acted out. The Milky Way was "the Castle of Gwydion". It was said that Gwydion pursued his sister, Arianrhod, down this path when he wanted her to "name, arm and marry" the child he had taken from her. Arianrhod had taken refuge in her star-castle, the delicate crown of stars which we call Corona Borealis. In early May meteor showers sometimes appear near this constellation. These shooting stars were believed to be souls returning to Earth to be reborn.

Stargazing

Go out on a clear starry night somewhere where there is minimal light pollution. Take a torch and a star-map. Lie on your back and look up. Find Corona Borealis (it is to the left of the constellation known as Boötes, the herdsman, which is just to the left of the Great Bear).

Imagine that you are being pulled up into the stars to visit the revolving castle of Arianrhod. This is a place where you can forget yourself for a moment in the bright darkness of the interstellar spaces. When you "come back to Earth", you will be reborn – a little different, and very much refreshed.

THE REALM OF THE BIRDS

The Celts believed that birds were the heralds of the Otherworld, and their song the speech of that realm, which we can *nearly* understand. In Welsh myth the birds of Rhiannon visit Bran's men as they carry their slain leader's severed head back from battle. Although the birds seem distant, their song sounds distinct and beautiful.

This describes accurately a phenomenon which occurs in lucid-dreaming – a strange, vivid alertness on the brink of sleep. Awareness of birds will sharpen your perceptions and allow fresh ideas to fly in through the windows of your mind.

The birds of Rhiannon

Listen out for the sounds of birds whether you are out walking or are sitting indoors. Listen not just to their song but also to the beating of their wings in the air, their rustles in the hedgerow. Birds are particularly loquacious at dawn and dusk. If you let your mind relax and focus your attention entirely on the birdsong, you will start to feel the boundaries between the kingdom of man and the realm of the birds dissolving, and you can almost understand what the birds have to tell you.

THE WHEEL OF THE YEAR

For the Celts the year was a wheel which rolled forward through the seasonal festivals, each with its special flavour and ceremonies. In early February the first snowdrops marked Imbolc, with the land thawing ready for the joyful quickening of Beltane, then building to midsummer, the summer's balance-point. In early August there would be Lammas games. Then, after harvest, the beasts would be fattened ready for slaughtering at Samhain. At this uncanny time the ancestors would be tapped for strength and inspiration to take the clan through the long dark of midwinter, back to the hopeful beginnings of spring.

Watching the wheel

The wheel doesn't just turn on itself, but also moves you forward, if you pay attention to the spirit of each festival and its opportunities.

This year, mark the festivals in a diary and celebrate them actively. Note your aims and observations at these times. Then you will be able to see how new ideas develop over the year, which seeds of inspiration germinate and which do not.

Understanding the rhythms of the year can help you lead a balanced and productive life, in tune with nature and the spirit of the time.

IMBOLC (FEBRUARY 1)

We celebrate Imbolc, or Candlemas, the Feast of Lights, at the time of the very first stirrings of spring, when the ewes start to give milk for the early lambs and the snowdrops are flowering. Imbolc also coincides with the feast day of St Brigit (known as Bride in Scotland). On the eve of the festival, Scottish girls would decorate a figure of Bride with shells, crystals and snowdrops, and carry it around their village. Then they would take her into a house, where they would bar the door and install the goddess in all her splendour. The young men of the village would humbly ask to see her. After they had made obeisance to her, there would be dancing and singing and at dawn the revellers would chant an invocation in honour of Bride.

The waking light

Get up just before dawn, light a candle, let its flame purify you and then put it before a mirror. Gaze into the mirror. Relax and allow the flickering flame to suggest images in your mind. They will tell you, in subtle ways, what is beginning to stir in you. Once the sky is light, go outside and welcome the new day.

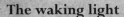

BELTANE (MAY 1)

Beltane is a celebration of spring, a rejoicing in the quickening and blossoming of the land. Many of the festivities of Beltane, such as dancing around the maypole and electing a May Queen, are still familiar to us, but others have largely been lost. For example, in the old days villagers would light a great fire made from the wood of nine sacred trees, and make their cattle jump over the fire to purify and protect the herd for the year ahead. Then, in some places, a special bannock (see recipe, opposite) was baked on the fire, broken up and handed round. Whoever got the most burned piece was the "sacrifice" and had to jump over the fire. In ancient times his or her fate may have been more sinister; but still, it's good to bear in mind the principle of sacrifice at Beltane – a time when everything seems possible but when it's easy to lose sight of the effort needed to achieve your aims.

Make a Beltane sacrifice

Beltane is the perfect time to throw away items you have hoarded over the winter. It is also a time to break free from comforting but restricting habits. What could you sacrifice to help yourself to blossom? Are there things that you like to do which consistently deflect you from achieving your aims? Write them down on a piece of paper.

Make a bonfire, pace or dance around it seven times, put the paper in the fire and watch it burn. If it's safe to do so, jump over the fire to end the ceremony.

A recipe for bannock

Ingredients (for 10 oatcakes):
140g/5oz rolled oats
110g/4oz plain flour
1 egg, beaten
55g/2oz sugar
150ml/5fl oz milk
½ tsp cinnamon
¼ tsp baking soda
½ tsp cream of tartar

Preheat a griddle over a medium heat — or on your Beltane bonfire. Mix the dry and wet ingredients separately in two large bowls. Then stir the wet into the dry gradually to avoid making lumps. Form the mixture into 10 small disks and cook them on the griddle until the edges become golden (about five minutes), turning once.

MIDSUMMER (JUNE 21)

At midsummer the sun reaches its zenith in the sky and we have the longest day and the shortest night – a potent time. In Cornwall all the hills around a certain bay would be crowned by bonfires on this night. Old people would read the future from the number and appearance of all the fires they could see. This is an axis-point in the year, a time when things can take a turn for the better – or worse. With this in mind some villages would hold sun-wise processions about the fields to ask the gods to protect the corn from drought or heavy rain.

A midsummer vigil

As a turning-point midsummer is an auspicious time to make decisions.

1 If the weather is good, sleep in the open, somewhere quiet yet brimming with earth energy. Before you go to sleep, say your intention out loud. Make sure you mean it!

2 Get up before sunrise and go to a spot where you can feel the rising sun filling you with its power. Once the sun is up, restate your intention.

3 Empty your mind and meditate before eating a hearty breakfast. Then take the next step toward making your intention happen.

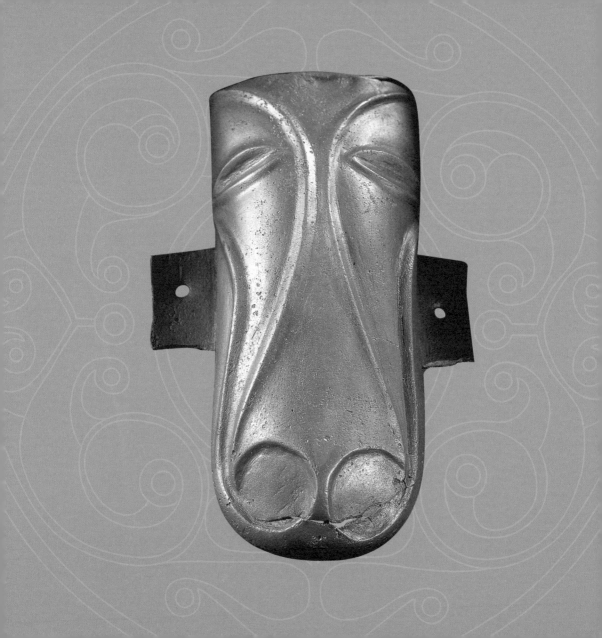

LAMMAS (AUGUST 1)

Lammas ("Loaf-mass") falls at the height of summer, when the crops are ripening and we are about to reap what we have sown. In Ireland big horse fairs and marriage markets are still held at this time. In the old days couples could "hand-fast" at Lammas for a year and a day. This was a trial marriage which could be dissolved if the couple didn't get on or conceive a child.

Lammas is also known as Lughnasa — the feast of Lugh, the solar god who is master of all skills. This is a time for celebrating your talents in friendly competition.

Fly a kite

Kite-flying is an ideal Lammas activity. Not only does it allow you to show your skill in controlling the kite, but it also takes you closer to the sun, and so to Lugh.

Among Lugh's many talents was that of craftsmanship, so, in his honour, try to make your own kite.

This isn't difficult, but it may require some practice.

Take your kite to a hill-top before dusk on Lammas-eve with friends. Bring some bread and local cheese and something to drink — home-made if possible. After flying your kite, eat and drink with your friends and watch the sun set.

SAMHAIN (NOVEMBER 1)

Samhain, literally "summer's end", is believed by some to be the start of the Celtic year. Just as day begins at night, so Samhain opens the door to the dark half of the year – when the light and life are draining from the world, we feel close to the dead and are keenly aware that we too one day will die.

At this time the Celts would slaughter animals, ready to dry or salt their meat for the winter. In the far past there may have been human sacrifice too, to honour the gods of the Otherworld. The presence of death and the fear of starvation in the coming months, sharpen the edge of consciousness and ripple the veil between the worlds.

If we stop to listen, we can commune with our ancestors and hear the wisdom of the Otherworld. This is a dark, ambiguous time when all sorts of roads, good and bad, that are normally barred to us are open for a brief spell. Some roads take us to the past, others to the future: Samhain is one of the most propitious times of the year to practise divination. Indeed, in Scotland those born at Samhain were said to have the "sight".

Telling winter tales

Before the industrial revolution, most people in the Celtic lands would spend cold evenings huddled in front of a fire, talking, making things and, above all, telling stories.

Sadly we have largely lost this tradition, but Samhain is a good time to rediscover it. Gather around the fire, drink cider punch with roasted apples floating in it, and tell tales full of mystery and terror. Don't be afraid to be afraid.

Mythic stories open up our sense of the possibilities of life, and what may lie beyond.

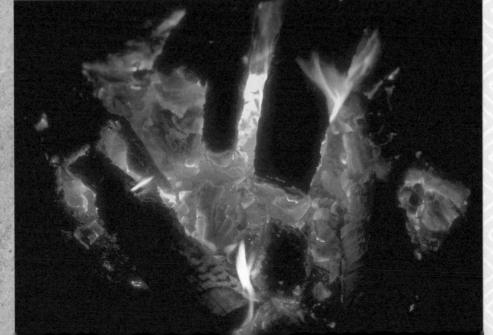

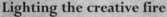

MIDWINTER (DECEMBER 21)

O n the longest night, especially in the far north of Europe when it is very long indeed, life can seem wretched and hopeless. The lack of daylight at this time makes many people feel depressed. In the northern isles too much drink is taken. But the sun does rise eventually and the days begin to lengthen. At midwinter we can use the darkness to dissolve outworn attitudes and defences, allow the tough old skin to slough off, and become as vulnerable and sensitive as a newborn child. Then, with the new light, real joy can arise.

Lighting the creative fire

Make a fire, inside or outside. Choose good kindling, such as tightly folded newspaper, to hold the flames, and use coal or wood as fuel so that the fire will burn well. Clear your mind, slow down your breathing and make a proper ceremony of lighting the fire. Sit and watch it burning for a while, letting your mind float freely. Let the flames burn away the dross, the outworn habits and thoughts, and clear a space for the new to seed itself in you. You do not have to know yet what the new will be. At Imbolc it will stir and show itself, and the wheel will keep turning.

MYSTIC SYMBOLS

From the motion-within-stillness of the endless knot, constructed on principles of cosmic geometry, to the stark simplicity of the cup or cauldron, the Celts wove a web of symbols which remind us that there is a deep and sometimes hidden meaning in the everyday. Whether you wear a triskele around your neck, stand before a Celtic cross or turn the pages of an illuminated gospel, you are on the threshold of the great mysteries that the druids, bards and saints knew. A little more contemplation will take you deep into the astonishing richness of the Celtic imagination.

BRIDGES BETWEEN WORLDS

The Celts' relish for the natural world was balanced by a longing for the serenity of the Otherworld. Symbols act as messengers or bridges between these two realms. A network of interlinked symbols gives shape and contour to a distinctively Celtic borderland. Some have probably arisen organically, others were invented by poets or mythmakers. Many hark back to old systems of mystical knowledge, now largely lost to us. By contemplating symbols we may gain access to this arcane wisdom, and unlock unexpected insights in ourselves.

Life-span

Tarr Steps in Devon, shown opposite, is believed to be the oldest bridge in Britain. It is also said to be a way to cross from the real world into the Otherworld.

In Welsh myth, Bran the Blessed makes a bridge of himself over the Irish Sea, so that his men can cross.

Like Bran, we are all capable of making bridges of ourselves, to enable others to cross over to truth or enlightenment. In what sense are *you* a bridge?

*"He who would be king,
let him first be a bridge."*

(FROM Bran's tale in the *Mabinogion*)

THE LABYRINTH

Labyrinths are found the world over, but the Celts particularly loved them – you can see this in their intricate curvilinear art which celebrates the experience of wandering widely but eventually returning to the source.

The labyrinth is symbolic of life's journey: as you travel onward you may forget where you have come from. It's easy to lose hold of the guiding threads of your purpose and principles. Sometimes you feel close to the centre but are actually far away, while sometimes you are close to your goal without realizing it.

The maze of the mind

It is often observed that the surface of the brain resembles a labyrinth. To get the most out of our mind, we need to stretch it in all ways, just as we need to travel all over the labyrinth to find its heart. Then the jewels of the brain start to glow and our mind "lights up".

Create a labyrinth

To draw a labyrinth or to make one, perhaps using stones on a beach, is a magical act which enlivens your mind. Start at the middle and work outward. Lose yourself in your task. When you emerge, you may be able to find a different approach to a troublesome problem.

RINGS, NECKLACES AND BRACELETS

Celtic tales are full of vivid description — of what people are wearing, the colour and richness of their hair, horses, cloaks and belt-buckles. As the Greek historian Strabo observed disapprovingly (below), the Celts cared about their appearance, enjoying the sensuality of fine clothes and precious jewelry.

Rings, necklaces and bracelets all encircle the flesh — they are a celebration of the body, a counterpoint to the asceticism of the Christian monks. Jewelry also conveyed status: the torc (opposite), worn around the neck, was the mark of a chieftain. The more gold a person wore, the more important they were.

Strabo on the Celts

"As well as simplicity and spiritedness, there is also much senselessness, boastfulness, and love of decoration in their nature. Not only do they often wear gold jewelry — in the shape of necklaces around their throats, and armlets and bracelets around their arms and wrists — but also those having an elevated rank wear garments that are brightly coloured and shot with gold."

(FROM Strabo's *Geography*)

Stepping out of the circle

It can be good to experiment with image and adornment, with degrees of visibility and invisibility. If you normally dress up and wear plenty of jewelry, just for one day do the opposite: wear plain clothes and no scent, make-up or jewelry. If you are normally scruffy or understated, for one day dress flamboyantly.

Do people treat you differently? Do you feel differently about yourself? Which elements of your new image do you intend to keep?

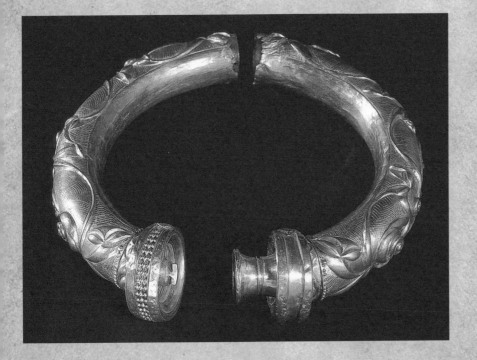

BOOKS AND LETTERS

The early Celts passed on their sacred knowledge, stories and myths orally, through generations of bards and Druids, but the Christians' holy revelations were contained in the Bible, and with Christianity came the book. The same scribes who lovingly copied out the gospels also wrote down the old myths and poems. This was both a gain and a loss: we have largely lost the "art of memory", but on the other hand priceless treasures of imagination and learning have been preserved for us as a source of inspiration and truth.

An appreciation of a book

A book is an object to be valued in its own right, not just for the message that it contains.

1 Choose a book that means a lot to you personally. Gaze on it closed, then slowly leaf through it until you find a page that draws you.

2 Contemplate the page without reading. Don't think or analyze, but instead enjoy with your inner senses the meaning the book has for you. Appreciate the beauty of the book in your mind's eye.

3 Close the book and give thanks to its creators.

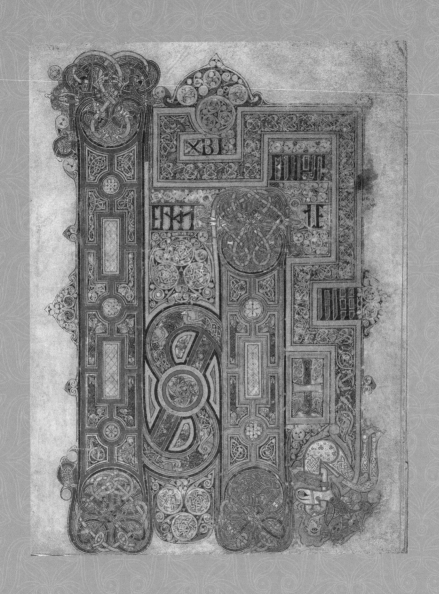

THE ILLUMINATED WORD

The Celts had a deep respect for the word – which they demonstrated in their love of riddles, poetry and story-telling. Indeed, to this day the people of the Celtic regions are noted for wit and verbal dexterity.

They were also talented artists – a flair they channelled into the making of the great illuminated gospels, such as the Book of Kells, the Lindisfarne Gospel and the Book of Durrow. Created between the sixth and eighth centuries by monks who devoted their lives to the work, they glorified the word in astonishing flowing, spiralling patterns whose jewelled colours still glow nearly 1,500 years later. Great pains were taken to source the raw materials required to produce such a stunning effect. For example, the blue pigment was made from powdered lapis lazuli, which had to be imported from Asia. The making of these books was a spiritual meditation which led the scribes into an intense and intimate relationship with the word of God.

Honour the word

Nowadays, printed text is commonplace. With such ready accessibility has come a loss of the sense of wonder at the written word that our Celtic ancestors would have felt. This exercise will help you to gain a renewed appreciation of the word.

1 Find a poem or text that inspires you. Copy it out onto fine-quality paper with a calligraphic pen. Concentrate on making your script as graceful as you can.

2 If you like you can elaborate your capitals and decorate the page with coloured figures and forms. Don't worry if your work doesn't look professional: a labour of love has its own beauty.

THE CELTIC CROSS

Although this ancient symbol was first found engraved on artefacts dating from 10,000 BC, it is said that St Patrick made the first Celtic cross in the fifth century AD. According to legend, he was shown a sacred standing stone marked with a circle to represent the moon goddess. Patrick made the mark of a Latin cross through the circle and blessed the stone. Thus was the lunar power of the old religion absorbed into solar Christianity. The emblem – a kind of Celtic yin-yang symbol – symbolizes the harmonious and dynamic union of opposites.

Sensing eternity

The cross stands for the earth, your body, the natural world, and all that you can smell, touch, taste, hear or see. The circle turns what seems to have a beginning and an end (such as a lifetime) into an endless cycle which exists in a dimension we cannot normally apprehend.

Close your eyes, bring to mind the image of the Celtic cross and focus on the "endless cycle" of your breathing. Breathe slowly, deeply and evenly. As your breathing becomes quieter and subtler, you may step out of your time-bound physical existence and enter the realm of eternity.

THE TREE OF LIFE

hen a tribe cleared the land for a settlement, they always left a great tree in the middle. This is where the chieftain would be inaugurated – for the tree, with its roots extending to the lower world and its branches reaching to the upper world, connected him with the power of both the heavens and the elements. In warfare tribes would try to destroy the mother tree of their enemies, to strip them of their identity and cut them off from the source of life.

Make friends with a tree

Making friends with a tree can reconnect us with the strength and simplicity of nature when we become anxious or confused.

1 Pick a tree that appeals to you whether in your garden, a park or woodland, and get to know it. You can sit, lie or exercise beneath it,

lean against it, climb into it, or just contemplate it from a distance.

2 Let the calm, powerful essence of the tree permeate your body and mind. Be particularly aware of how the roots penetrate deep into the earth and the branches reach up into the sky. Your own being will relax and expand in sympathy.

MAGICAL ANIMALS

In the early Celtic world, humans depended for their survival on the animals they herded or hunted. This close relationship was the inspiration for the many helpful and magical animals that appear in the myths. In the Welsh tale of Culwych and Olwen, Arthur's band of heroes are helped in their quest to rescue an imprisoned boy, Mabon, by the four "oldest animals": the stag, the owl, the eagle and the salmon. These animals have existed down the ages, since before humans, and are blessed with a wisdom and goodness not possessed by humankind. The owl says: "When first I came hither, the wide valley you see was a wooded glen. And a race of men came and rooted it up." The ancient salmon knows where the missing boy is, so he takes two of the heroes "on his two shoulders" to the walls of the prison and carries them into attack, so that the boy is rescued.

Some animals, such as the hare, were considered so magical and uncanny that they were taboo, and so could not be eaten. For example, people believed that witches turned themselves into hares to steal milk from cows. And when Boudicca, queen of the Celtic tribe the Iceni, stood with her army facing the Romans for the first time, she made an augury by letting a hare out from under her skirts and watching the direction in which it ran. She predicted victory and did indeed win that battle, although she later lost the war.

Animal powers

Watch the animals you encounter and notice the qualities they possess that we lack – the unquestioning loyalty of the dog, the nimbleness of the squirrel, the owl's amazing hearing and eyesight. Choose one and try to develop it in yourself. Imagine yourself in the animal's body and view the world through its eyes. For example, the next time you're delayed, don't feel frustrated – instead, think yourself into the tranquil patience of the cat.

TALISMANS

The most famous talismans or magical instruments in Celtic tradition are the "Four Hallows" which the magical Tuatha Dé Danaan, "the children of the Goddess Danu", brought to Ireland: the Sword of Nuadu, the Spear of Lugh, the Cauldron of the Daghda and the Stone of Destiny. These are thought to be central to the well-being and destiny of the Celtic lands.

Talismans usually protect or assist the virtuous, but they also show up the failings of undeserving people who try to use them. For example, the Whetstone of Tudwal Tudgyd will sharpen the sword of a brave man but blunt that of a coward; while the Mantle of Tegau Golden Breast will only hang in proper, natural folds on a woman of good character.

Create a talisman

With a little imagination, you can create a talisman for yourself or for someone in need.

1 First, decide what you are going to use. It could be any beautiful or intriguing object, as long as it is meaningful to you, but a stone, a gem or a piece of carved wood would be particularly suitable.

2 Charge the object up by holding it against different parts of your body while meditating: the heart for emotional strength, the forehead for mental clarity, the belly for power.

3 Put the talisman into a silk bag. If it is to be a gift, offer it with love, stating its purpose – for example, "This is to give you alertness and courage for your upcoming test."

Power of the hallows

The Lady's gifts to the western ones,
Cauldron and sword, spear and stone;
The Lady's words, over the foam,
Blessings to all when my fair Lord comes.

(ANONYMOUS)

THE TWISTED VINE

If you look closely at the patterns on illuminated manuscripts and on Celtic stone crosses you will often see rooted in a golden chalice a vine which twists and twines and provides bunches of grapes for peacocks with iridescent tail feathers. Christ was the "true vine" and the grapes represent the fruits of his life which are always there to feed the faithful. The golden bowl stands for the promise of redemption and the dazzling outspread tails of the peacocks represent the Resurrection. The symbolism resonates at a deep level of the unconscious.

A vine-like power

The vine grows in a particularly determined manner. It can bind itself to a wall or wrap around a tree. It combines flexibility and firmness as it climbs upward.

Seek inspiration from the vine at times when you can feel your resolve wavering – for example, if you're battling against a long illness or enduring any other sustained period of stress.

Close your eyes and focus on your solar plexus. Allow energy to rise from here into your upper body and head, like a vine climbing toward the sun. Sense renewed confidence and strength coursing through you.

THE ENDLESS KNOT

The Celts were fascinated by the symbol of the endless knot – an elaborately interlaced line without a starting or finishing point. The knot is a kind of Celtic mandala, a cosmic mind-map. It expresses the Celts' belief in eternity – a transcendental state beyond the material world.

Meditate on the eternal truth
Meditate on the endless knot as the ultimate reality of the cosmos, the eternal truth of existence, the immortality of the spirit.

1 Sit comfortably with the endless knot in front of you. Breathe evenly and deeply.

2 Focus your awareness on the endless knot. Let the image seep into your consciousness.

3 Don't attempt to put your thoughts into words, but just sit there, with the knot in your mind, calmly experiencing the present, sensing time as a continual flow inseparably linked with eternity. Stay like this for five to ten minutes.

4 End your meditation by repeating to yourself seven times the following affirmation: "Each moment is a curve on the endless knot of time."

THE CAULDRON

In early times the cauldron sat over the fire, and meat, bones, vegetables and herbs would simmer in a sustaining broth. The rich stew in the cauldron became a potent symbol for the Celts, for spiritual as well as physical nourishment – for inspiration, mystic knowledge, and regeneration. Dead warriors who plunge into Bran's cauldron come back to life but without the power of speech – signifying that you can't talk about the great mysteries, they can only be experienced or tasted. And when little Gwion tastes the brew in Cerridwen's cauldron, he begins the journey that transforms him into the all-knowing bard Taliesin.

A cauldron of transformation

When you're facing a period of difficult change, find or make a cauldron. It doesn't have to be big, but it should have a round, embracing shape, like a bowl.

Put into the cauldron any negative emotion you need to transform – for example, disappointment, fear, resentment or guilt. Look into the cauldron and imagine it drawing this quality from you. Pour in some water or wine and swill it around, then take a sip. Trust in the process of transformation: let it happen without any further input from you.

THE CUP

The cup or goblet is a female symbol. In Irish legend it is associated with Maeve, goddess of sovereignty and intoxication. Each new king of Ireland would have to "marry" Maeve to assume the throne. A priestess (taking on the role of the goddess) would offer a cup containing the "ale of cuala" to the new king. By drinking from the cup – and, in ancient times, by sleeping with the priestess – he signified his willingness to marry the land and become its guardian.

To drink from the Celtic cup means not just that you commune with the one who offers it, but that you dedicate yourself to the service of the higher powers that it represents.

Offering the cup

You can make a magic drink from a sweet herb (such as lime-flower, camomile or meadowsweet), honey and, if you like, a little whisky. Offer it to your partner or friend in the spirit of love and mutual empowerment. Allow the other person to drink, then take the cup and drink yourself.

This simple, intimate ceremony signifies a promise to be true to what is best and most noble in your relationship.

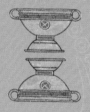

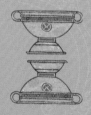

THE GRAIL

The Grail is neither cup nor cauldron but something on a higher level than either. It has its roots in the Celtic tradition, as a magic vessel in which the dew of the Otherworld gathered. When, later, it acquired a Christian meaning – as the Holy Grail in which Joseph of Arimathea collected the blood of Christ at the Crucifixion – it was tirelessly sought by the knights of King Arthur's round table, such as Galahad and Perceval. Some people believe that it has the power to heal all mankind and can be seen only by those who are pure of heart. Its origins may be unclear, but the Grail has become a powerful symbol of whatever is most precious, elusive and meaningful to each of us.

The Grail meditation

Sit in a quiet place with your back straight and neck relaxed. Let your breathing settle. Allow an image of the Grail to arise in your mind. Experience the Grail with your inner senses: how does it feel to the touch, what substance is within it, does it ring when struck?

Call on the subtle power of this great symbol to reaffirm your connection with the source of life.

THE HEAD

For the Celts, the head was where a person's soul resided. Enemies' severed heads were set up on poles, and the dying command of Bran the Blessed was for his head to be buried, facing France, under the White Mount at the Tower of London, to protect Britain from invasion. For 80 years Bran's men carried his head as a talisman before fulfilling his wish. Some believe that it is still buried under the Tower like the seed of sovereignty, still keeping Britain from harm.

Enliven your head

This exercise is intended to enhance your intellect and imagination.

1 Sit in the dark and contemplate a lighted candle – placed inside a pumpkin-head lantern, if you like.

2 Become aware of the light at the centre of your own head. Then of the space behind your eyes. Of the two "dragon's wings" which the sides of your brain make. Of the dragon's tail which runs from the back of your head down your spine.

3 Allow your breath to travel into these spaces. Imagine your mind-dragon breathing fire into your endeavours.

THE SWORD OF LIGHT

The sword used by the Irish hero Fergus mac Roich was called Caladbolg – from the words "calad" (hard) and "bolg" (lightning). Fergus performed mighty deeds with his sword of light. He was even able to use it to shape the Irish landscape, as described in the quotation below.

A sword of light is no ordinary weapon: it cannot be used for indiscriminate slaughter, but only for fighting on the side of good. Swords of the power of Caladbolg can be wielded only by the strongest and most noble warriors such as Arthur, Rhydderch, and Luke Skywalker – a modern-day hero in the Celtic tradition, whose sword-blade really is a beam of light.

Carving the landscape

Whenever Fergus desired to strike with Caladbolg, it became the size of a rainbow in the air. Thereupon Fergus turned his hand slantwise over the heads of the hosts, so that he cut the tops off the three hills. They can still be seen on the moor, and these are the three Maels of Meath.

(FROM THE *Táin Bó Cúailnge*)

The flash of inspiration

Inspiration can come in a lightning flash, but sometimes our minds are working too slowly to register the message. And perhaps we also subconsciously shy away from the transformative effect of a great idea.

We need to learn to be receptive to these glimpses and flashes, which are so often discarded and drowned out by the rational forebrain.

One way of doing this is to drift into sleep mindfully. Try to be aware of the moment when your consciousness shifts. This isn't easy, but even if you manage it only occasionally you will be able to watch the brain speed up and jump into an extraordinarily creative mode. Afterwards you should be more sensitive to these "flashes of inspiration" when they occur.

HEROES OF THE SPIRIT

Celtic myth and history have brought many great heroes and heroines into the world — noble but flawed Lancelot, brave Boudicca and ferocious Cuchulainn, questing seafarers such as Brendan and Maelduin, vigorous magic-wielding saints such as Brigit and Columba. In their grand, sometimes tragic lives we see our own writ large, and there is much to learn from their adventures and destinies. When the stressful complexities of modern life conspire to make us fearful or sad we can remember the Celtic spirit of exploration, and the impulse that goes with it to live a big and worthwhile life.

THE HEROIC VOCATION

The Celts believed that you must fulfil your destiny, and be prepared to fight for it if necessary. Then your honour will be bright and your name and deeds celebrated by the bards. Heroes and heroines often learn very early that they have a special vocation. In Celtic legend Cuchulainn knew that he would die young, but before he did he earned the right to call himself the "best warrior in the western world". Until he pulled the sword out of the stone, Arthur was an ordinary boy who had no sense of his special role. His destiny was thrust upon him – by taking possession of his sword, Excalibur, Arthur announced to himself and to those around him that he was to be the "once and future king".

A sense of destiny also played its part in the imagined lives of historical figures. The radiant light emanating from her baby's room tells St Columba's mother that he is a holy child, and the boy grows up to be a pioneer of Christianity in Scotland and to found the island monastery of Iona, which is still a lighthouse of inspiration for the Celtic Christians.

Following your destiny

Heroes and heroines set themselves
apart by following their destiny
with courage and conviction. It is
more rewarding to be true to
yourself and your calling than
to chase the short-term benefits
offered by conformity.

If you're prepared to hear the
answers, meditate on questions such
as: Who am I? What am I here for?
You may need to make a journey
to a place of power to ask these
questions. Don't expect the answers
to come in a certain way, or to
appeal to your ego: be open to the
unexpected. And be ready to live
with the knowledge, whatever it
may be. There's always a price to
pay for following your destiny –
are you willing to pay it?

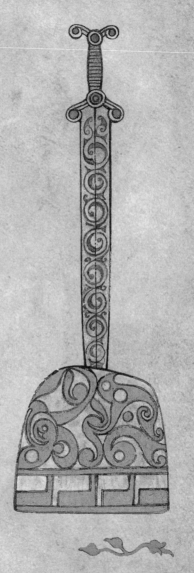

THE WAY OF THE WARRIOR

The arts of war were taken very seriously by the Celts. Boys were subjected to a rigorous training in the use of sword, spear, bow and dirk. They also developed ways of unnerving the enemy, such as Cuchulainn's famous salmon-leap. A Celtic warrior had no fear of death because he believed that his soul was immortal. Battle was a magical act performed in a state of altered consciousness, sometimes induced by alcohol.

Courage, honour and skill were paramount: if anyone impugned his name, a warrior would fight his challenger to the death. Better to die with honour than to live a coward's life.

The invisible sword

The best warriors don't have to fight, because their aura commands respect. Use this exercise when you are confronted by an adversary.

1 Breathe into your backbone – feel it strong and straight, like a sword. Picture this sword moving forward so that it hangs before you. Channel your breath into the sword to make it glow with light.

2 Holding this image in your mind, stand your ground calmly and without aggression.

THE QUEST

In the Arthurian knights' quest for the Grail, purity and goodness count for more than brute strength. The search takes place within the souls of the questors. The Fisher King, who guards the Grail, has sustained a grievous wound in the groin, which will not heal and which has also caused the land to be laid to waste. The knights must experience the mystery of the Grail to heal the kingdom and the king – or all is lost.

Like Lancelot, Galahad, Perceval and their fellow knights, we often begin a personal quest as a response to adversity. It is as if our suffering gives us the courage and vision to explore, take risks and live a bigger, braver life.

Soul searching

Take time to review your life, weighing up the good and the bad. Celebrate your achievements, and also think about the things you have wanted to do for many years but have not yet accomplished. What are these things? You still have time to do them.

Choose the most important and consider what the first step toward fulfilling this goal would be.

Write down the step and vow, on your honour as a warrior, to take it.

SPIRITUAL PIONEERS

The knights of Arthur's round table take on the role of spiritual adventurers in their quest for the Grail. But many of these brave and wise men do not find what they seek, because their pride and ambition are too great. In contrast young Perceval (whose name means "pierce-the-veil") has been brought up by his widowed mother deep in the forest, and has never seen a knight, or a sword, or even a horse. He is ill-clad, unlettered, and entirely lacking in the chivalric graces expected of a knight, yet his innocence leads him in a spirit journey to the Grail, which has eluded so many. However, when he sees the Grail, he forgets to ask "Whom does the Grail serve?", the mysterious question that will heal the Fisher King and the wasted land. When he awakes, his vision is gone.

We all have moments when we sense the great truths of existence, but then we become entangled in our everyday lives and forget these shafts of wisdom. The spiritual adventurer explores the borderlands between Heaven and Earth where the Grail is to be found. You must develop a calm, quiet heart in the midst of a noisy, distracting world. Only then can you hope to lay your hands on the Grail.

The riddle of the Grail

The question that the Grail knights had to ask was "Whom does the Grail serve?" This cannot be answered by the brain alone: you also need to be sensitive to the subtle messages of your intuition.

You could begin by asking "Whom or what do I serve?" It may be that you serve yourself, in which case you might ask who this "self" is.

The Grail question is a Celtic riddle of the highest order which can take a lifetime to solve.

SEAFARING

The Celts living on the western edge of Europe had a strong feeling for the sea. They believed that if you set sail westward you would reach the "Isles of the Blessed", where the apple tree of Emain yielded its golden apples. The tales of these sea voyages, called *immrama*, can be seen as a metaphor for the journey of the soul after death, toward the dark islands in the setting sun where our true home lies.

The thrill of departure

Many Irish and Scots Celts were forced by hunger or landlessness to leave their homelands and sail to the New World. This felt like a kind of death for them – but actually a great adventure awaited them as they helped to found America. If you have to leave somewhere or someone you love, you may find this visualization helpful.

Imagine you are looking down on the scene of a large ship preparing for a long journey. The crowd on the quay are restless, the passengers hanging over the rails are weeping one moment and laughing the next. Ask yourself: would you rather stay behind or go? Once the decision to go is made, and you begin to let go of the old ways, departure can be a supremely exhilarating experience.

WISE WOMEN AND WIZARDS

W ise magicians of both sexes play an intriguing part in Celtic myth, helping heroes to fulfil their destiny by training, guiding and supporting them. The most famous is Merlin, the "child with no father" who solves the riddle of the red and white dragons fighting beneath the Welsh mountains. He tells the king, Vortigern, that the red dragon stands for the Britons and the white for the Saxons – and that the Britons will prevail in the end. Merlin goes on to devise the challenge of the sword in the stone and then becomes King Arthur's counsellor.

Scathach is the teacher and seeress who turns Cuchulainn into the "best warrior in the western world". The Irish hero comes to her fortress on the Isle of Skye, which he reaches by crossing a treacherous bouncing bridge, and he then has to overpower the formidable Scathach. Once he has managed this she agrees to teach him all the secrets of the Celtic martial arts. Before sending him on his way, she consults an oracle and tells his fortune: she sees blood, slaughter and victory lying ahead of him, a life full of love which is to end when he is 33 years old.

Consult your inner counsellor

If you dream of a helpful or wise figure, you can turn him or her into an inner counsellor who can help you in your waking life as well.

1 To cue such a dream, you must incubate an image of your inner counsellor. Give them a name and visualize their physical appearance as clearly as possible.

2 Once this person has been imprinted in your unconscious, you can bring him or her to mind when you need guidance, and have a conversation with them about your problem. Write this dialogue down so that you can think hard about what they have to say. You may be surprised and impressed by the wisdom that emerges in this way.

KINGS AND QUEENS

The Celtic ruler had to be a champion of truth, harsh to the wicked and gentle to the weak. It was vitally important that the right person take the crown because he or she would become a channel for the supernatural powers of Heaven and must be strong to avoid being broken by them. At Tara in Ireland, when Conaire was installed as High King, there was a series of ritual trials that he had to pass through: he had to put on a mantle that would fit only the true king; he had to drive a chariot pulled by two horses of the same colour that had never before been harnessed; and when he did so, two flagstones would open to allow the chariot through and the Lia Fail, the Stone of Destiny, would screech against its axle.

Truth in a ruler

Truth in a ruler is as bright as the foam cast up by a mighty wave, as the sheen of a swan in the sun, as the colour of snow on a mountain. A ruler's truth is an effort that overpowers armies. It brings milk into the world, it brings corn and mast.

(EARLY IRISH TEXT)

The Celtic queen

Celtic queens were often powerful women in their own right, not merely the consorts of kings. In East Anglia, Boudicca led her army into many campaigns against the Romans after they had humiliated her and raped her daughters – and nearly won victory. Queen Cartimandua, on the other hand, was a canny politician who chose to make peace with the Romans and ruled for 40 years in northern England.

The queens of Elfland, celebrated in the old ballads and poems, are Otherworld rulers who tempt men into their realm, initiate them into the sexual mysteries and empower them as seers and wizards. This is an aspect of the queen as Goddess of Sovereignty who gives the chosen king the power to rule the land.

The inner king and queen

The sacred marriage of the king and queen can be seen as the fusion of the male and female poles in our psyche which is necessary to make us dynamic and complete human beings. But we often have difficulty understanding the opposite sex, which can limit our creativity and cause disagreements with partners and lovers. For one week try acting toward members of the opposite sex with the utmost consideration. You don't need to follow courtly codes of conduct, but, if you act in the right spirit, you will find positive changes happening in both your inner and your outer world.

Wise use of power

The aspects of our personality, our different "I"s, are like the subjects in a kingdom – one "I" may want one thing, while another may want something quite different. If you have ever tried to give up smoking, lose weight or make other changes in your habits, you will know the truth of this. The trick is to govern these different parts of yourself judiciously, as a wise king or queen does his or her subjects. To do this you need an overview.

1 Go to a high place – ideally one with a view over a rural landscape. The elevated setting will give you a heightened sense of self and will still your mind as you contemplate the harmony of nature.

2 Look down on your life as objectively as you can. What are the unruly parts of yourself – and how can they be controlled without warfare? What are your strong points and how can you make better use of them? Might the energy of the unruly "I"s be harnessed for some creative purpose? Your inner sovereign may see a way to do this.

3 As you walk back down from the high place, consider how to apply any insights you have gained.

SAINTS AND ANGELS

C eltic saints were singularly bold and adventurous characters, whose miraculous powers had more than a touch of druidical magic in them. St Columba of Iona was an exceptionally holy man with clairvoyant gifts and an intimate relationship with angels. According to legend, an angel came to his mother before his birth to announce that she was carrying a special child, and, as he grew up, it is said that he was accompanied everywhere by an angel.

St Brigit of Kildare, still much loved in Ireland as "the Mary of the Gaels", also possessed unusual powers: when she was a young woman, her stepbrothers were putting pressure on her to marry, so she knocked out one of her eyes to discourage the prospective suitor. Once her family decided to allow her to remain a virgin, she was miraculously able to restore the sight of the eye.

Perhaps because the early Celts admired both boldness and wizardry, the legends about Celtic saints tend to emphasize these qualities rather than humility or piety.

Be my light, be my guide

There is a strong Celtic tradition
of calling on saints for help in
moments of dire suffering or need,
and many people have a particular
saint whom they love and trust.

If this idea appeals to you, read
about the lives of the Celtic saints.
Is there one with whom you feel
a particular affinity? Seek comfort
from your saint, as he or she
watches over your actions. Invoke
their name in blessings for your
loved ones, as in the example below.

Be the cowl of Columba over thee,
Be the cowl of Michael militant
  about thee,
Christ's cowl, beloved, safeguard thee,
The cowl of the God of grace
  safeguard thee.

(FROM THE *Carmina Gadelica*)

INDEX

ACKNOWLEDGMENTS

The publisher would like to thank the following individuals, museums, and photographic libraries for permission to reproduce their material. Every care has been taken to trace copyright holders. However, if we have omitted anyone we apologize and will, if informed, make corrections to any future edition.

Key
AA: The Art Archive
BAL: Bridgeman Art Library
RHPL: Robert Harding Picture Library
WFA: Werner Forman Archive

page 2 AA/British Library; **7** Homer Sykes/Corbis; **14–15** Trustees of The British Museum; **16** Steve Austin/Papilio/Corbis; **21** Kevin Fleming/Corbis; **22–23** Trustees of The British Museum; **30** Darrell Gulin/Corbis; **35** WFA/National Museum of Ireland; **38** Getty Images; **40–41** WFA/National Museum of Copenhagen; **45** C.M. Dixon; **53** WFA/The British Museum; **55** Adam Woolfitt/Corbis; **60** Bernard Annebicque/Corbis/Sygma; **62–63** Image State; **65** Guy Edwards/Natural History Photographic Agency; **73** Nick Haslam/Hutchison Library; **76** Tizianna and Gianni Baldizzone/Corbis; **79** Hans Strand/Corbis; **80** Adam Woolfitt/Corbis; **87** Image State; **88** D. Beatty/RHPL; **92** Image State; **94** WFA/The British Museum; **97** Todd A. Gipstein/Corbis; **98** Randy O'Rourke/Corbis; **100–101** Chrisopher J. Morris/Corbis; **103** E.O. Hoppe/Corbis; **107** WFA/National Museum of Ireland; **109** AKG Images; **112** Tim Thompson/Corbis; **125** Württembergisches Landesmuseum, Stuttgart; **126** Trustees of the British Museum; **131** AA; **134–135** BAL/Simon Marsden; **139** Réunion des Musées Nationaux/Jean Schormans; **141** AKG Images; **144** Richard Cummins/Corbis; **153** AA